BREATHE
DEEP

BREATHE
DEEP

30 DAYS OF ENCOUNTERING GOD

IN THE MYSTERIES AND TENSIONS

OF LIFE AND FAITH

SARA KATARINA

ISBN: 978-1-7781035-1-3 (e-book)

978-1-7781035-0-6 (paperback)

Thank you for buying my book! To say "thanks", I would like to send you 3 free downloadable wallpapers! Simply e-mail authorsarakatarina@gmail.com or sign up to be a part of my e-mail list at the QR code below or at authorsarakatarina.weebly.com

To: Nana, Papa, Oma and Opa.
Who have believed in me from the very beginning.

CONTENTS

PREFACE

This devotional book may not be like others you have encountered. Before you dive into the content of this devotional, I want to provide a quick overview of what this book is all about. This book is all about asking questions. My prayer is that as you go through these 30 devotionals you would encounter God in the mystery. A lot of these devotionals have to do with processing pain, and this is intentional. It is not about finding answers to pain, but about finding the God who cares in the middle of it. Each day begins with a poem for you to read and reflect on. Some people might want to stop there, and that's fine! For those wanting to enter more of a conversation surrounding the poem, I have included a discussion explaining some of the things I have learned and questions I have and still am wrestling through. Following each discussion are a couple of questions for reflection. I would encourage you to use these questions as starting points for a conversation with yourself, God, or others. Finally, at the end of each day there is a prayer. These prayers are also meant to be starting points of conversation between you and God. Join me in wrestling in the tension to grow closer to a God who is always there, especially when we don't feel like it.

DAY ONE

The Valley of Fallen Leaves

My heart is overwhelmed with love and grace.
How unworthy I feel,
But here I am—
I with You and
You with me
As I walk through
The Valley of Fallen Leaves
Of Fallen Dreams.
All it takes
Is for someone
To pick up that leaf
To pick up that dream
To make it into something beautiful.
Maybe leaves weren't meant
To only be green.
Maybe dreams weren't meant
To only be dreams.
With a little imagination,
A leaf can be changed into something different.
With a little inspiration,
A dream can be changed
In order to make a difference.
Bring the words of praise to my lips.
Help me to reclaim Your dream
As I walk through the Valley
Of Fallen Leaves
Of Fallen Dreams.

DISCUSSION

Have you ever walked along a path in autumn, with trees all around you and the ground coated in colorful leaves that crunch under your feet while you walk? I love finding these paths and enjoying them while they last. The color of the leaves and that satisfying crunch as I step on them is an indicator that winter is coming. Somehow, the season between the end of summer and the beginning of winter is such a beautiful time, even though the end of summer and the start of winter can be a dreary thing.

I love this in-between moment of time because it sparks something new. Even though the dark of winter is approaching, there is something about autumn that just seems magical. I've found that sometimes my dreams can be like that. And by dreams, I mean the things I want to do with my life. Oftentimes things do not go the way I would have expected as I walk towards achieving a dream. Plans change, people change, and suddenly, my dream seems to be falling like leaves. There is sadness in the loss or change of a dream, and time to grieve is important. But like autumn, there can also be hope as I realize that like a leaf, I can pick up the fragments of my fallen dream and use them as inspiration to start a new dream. The impact cannot be seen right away, and like a leaf found in a book years later, sometimes a dream needs to be tucked away for a while. When the dream is rediscovered, the possibilities to achieve it are new and fresh. Everyone will experience a dream that has fallen apart. That valley can be a sad place. That valley can also be a place of hope.

QUESTIONS FOR REFLECTION

Which dreams of yours have fallen? What inspiration could you use to pick them up and make a new dream?

PRAYER

God of the Valley of Fallen Dreams, this is a hard place to be. We see our dreams falling and we want to believe they can be formed into something new. But it's hard to see that sometimes. Help us to find inspiration for new dreams among the leaves. Amen.

Breathe

I'm nervous;
Just breathe.
I'm hurting;
Just breathe.
I'm scared;
Just breathe.
I'm at peace;
Just breathe.
I'm joyful;
Just breathe.
I'm enjoying the moment;
Just breathe.
Why?
Because it is vital.
It helps you to enjoy life;
It gives you perspective.
But what about when it hurts?
Breathe deeper.
But that hurts more.
With every breath I take
My heart breaks.
If I don't breathe,
The pain stops.
Life is beautiful
But breathing is painful.
Just breathe.

DISCUSSION

"Just breathe." These are common words usually spoken with the same intention as "seize the day" or "enjoy every moment." Breathing is a vital aspect of staying alive. You have likely taken CPR courses that teach you what to do should a person stop breathing. Maybe you remember playing the "how long can you hold your breath" game as a kid, and the fact that you are reading this book means that at some point you started to breathe again. When life is mundane and ordinary, I usually don't think about breathing too much; it's natural and my body just does it. However, in seasons of pain, I find myself very aware of each breath I take.

I've been told each breath is a gift, but on days when I'm feeling emotional pain, each breath seems to hurt. Maybe I am the only one who has this kind of experience sometimes. And then there are other times when life seems to be going great and I just want to absorb it all, and again I am very aware of the breaths that I take in those moments. The phrase "just breathe" to me means more than the act of breathing; it means taking a moment, a couple of seconds, to slow down and analyze or absorb what is happening around me. And sometimes it is hard to take a deep breath and slow down for those couple seconds because what is happening around me or in me is painful and I would rather not think about it. But I find that if I don't slow down and breathe in the hard moments, I also don't slow down and breathe in the good moments. Physical breathing is an unconscious habit. Giving yourself space to emotionally breathe is a formed habit.

QUESTIONS FOR REFLECTION

What are the moments in your life where you catch yourself taking a second to breathe? Are these good or painful moments? How can you develop a habit of emotional breathing?

PRAYER

Breathe in and say to yourself, "Peace." Breathe out and say to yourself, "Be still."

Pain

Why is pain so real?
Why does it hurt so much?
Why is it so hard?
Why is it so easy to trust in pain?
Why is pain internal?
Why can't pain be explained?
Why does pain increase dependence?
Why is pain worth it?
Why is pain relentless?
Why is pain effective?
Why is pain scary?
Why is pain confusing?
Why is pain silent?
Why is pain exhausting?
Why is pain beautiful?
Why is pain ugly?

Pain is hard because it hurts.
Pain is easy because of complacency.
Pain is beautiful because of the result.
Pain is ugly because of the process.

What is pain?
Pain is the springboard to relationship.

DISCUSSION

Every experience of pain is unique. I wrote this poem during a time when I was dealing with a lot of emotional pain, and these questions entered my mind often. Every answer I received seemed to be superficial. Phrases like, "it's for the best," "it will make you stronger," "God knows what He is doing," left me feeling so alone and like I should somehow be grateful for this pain, and if I wasn't, then I didn't have enough faith. On the other side of pain, it is sometimes possible to say these things, but when you are in pain, these words cut your heart. I was tired of feeling hurt by these answers, and so I stopped talking about my pain. What I realize now is that my pain was a springboard to my relationship with God.

I don't believe God causes pain, and that means He was with me in the middle of mine. I found verses like Isaiah 43:2 to be so comforting because they spoke about God being present in the pain. I was not alone in my silence. God became someone safe to talk to because He never told me to "just have more faith" or "pray more." He was simply with me, and even when I didn't feel it to be true, I chose to believe it because it gave me hope. I dove into the prophets of the Old Testament and found myself in their stories. God's called and chosen, experiencing pain and being honest with Him about it. These stories anchored me in a God whom I don't fully understand but I know is with me and cares for me, even when it may look and feel the opposite. Eventually, I did let people into my pain, and I discovered that while some responded in ways like those who did before, most let me in on some sort of pain they were struggling with too. I truly am not alone. These conversations on the frustrations and the hardship and the hope we choose to have in pain led to some lasting friendships. And it was all made possible by pain.

QUESTIONS FOR REFLECTION

Where in your life is there pain? How do you think it could be a springboard to relationship?

PRAYER

God who is present in pain, when we go through pain, we need You to be with us. We need to know Your presence is real. You are the Lord, the Holy God, and we often don't understand why we are going through this. You call us precious and honoured, O God we want to believe it. Remind us that we are loved, even when we are in pain. Amen.
(Prayer adapted from Isaiah 43:2–4)

Confessions

We all have confessions to make,
Things we don't want anyone to know,
Thoughts of harm,
Thoughts of what the world would be like without us.
Emotionally, we beat ourselves up.
We strive for perfection
But we always, always fail,
And when that happens,
Our thoughts turn against us.
We become so broken
That it is difficult to breathe—
Guilt and shame consume us
And we cannot seem to stop.
And so, we spiral.
We get so bruised and tired
That we don't know how to ask for help
Because we are afraid—
Afraid that when someone finds out
They will treat us differently.
Our damaged soul will be
A weight that no one wants to bear.
We want to stop but we can't.
A call out to God and things might get better
But then the thoughts come back again.
Truth can be found
But we still can't stop.
We need to discover truth

Before we can understand it,
But there's a disconnect.
Jesus, show us what to do—
Help our hearts to understand Your truth.
These confessions we don't want to make
Need to be spoken.
Jesus loves us.
May we learn to love ourselves.

DISCUSSION

I wrote this poem at the lowest point of my life. I didn't know what to do with all my emotional pain. I felt like because the pain wasn't physical, it somehow didn't matter. When I tried to talk about it, I felt like I wasn't taken seriously. I knew the truth of how much God and my family loved me, but it still didn't seem to make a difference in how I felt or how I thought. There would be seasons where the pain seemed to go away and the destructive thoughts stopped, but then they would come back again, and I would feel like such a failure. I thought it was my effort that would heal me, because when I called out to God, nothing changed for long.

When I wrote this poem, I told myself I would never show it to anyone. It was too embarrassing, too personal, and too messy for anyone else to understand. But I share it now because I have found hope and I have found a way to stop the spiral. Those thought patterns no longer consume me. I have reached a place where I can share this dark moment of my life because I know there are others who are there right now. You feel alone and afraid and like no one could possibly understand what you are going through. Let me start by saying everyone's pain is unique, so, no, I don't know exactly how you feel. But if you can relate in any way to this poem, I want you to know there is hope even though everything seems so dark.

I found this confession especially hard to make in church circles because I didn't exhibit joy all the time and I questioned the goodness of God a lot. Over time, I realized that the mark of a Christian is not an emotion of joy. The Psalms are full of prayers questioning God's presence and His justice. There is freedom to ask questions, and as I wrestled with God through these things, I found Him in my questions. No, I did not get all the answers, but I learned to trust God with what I don't know. Because here's the thing about wrestling, you can't wrestle with someone without being close to them. In the wrestling, I found hope, help, and healing. And there came a point when I needed to let others in. You do not have to walk through these things alone. Be patient with yourself and allow others to walk with you through these hard times.

QUESTIONS FOR REFLECTION

Is there pain in your life you are hiding from others? Can you imagine what your life would look like without this pain? Who is the person in your life you could make your confession too? * *If you cannot think of anyone, start with telling God.*

PRAYER

God of Emotion, thank You for giving us examples of people who questioned Your goodness and walked through dark valleys. Thank You for loving us even when we don't realize or don't know how to get better. May we find You in the wrestling. Protect us from ourselves. Amen.

Worth It

You're worth it.
You're worth the pain.
You're worth My scars.
I went willingly to the cross to take your pain and
exchange it for My healing.
To take your sin and exchange it for My righteousness.
To take your insecurities and exchange them for My
peace.
To take your weakness and exchange it for My strength.
To take your bitterness and exchange it for My hope.
To take your loneliness and exchange it for My presence.
Just sit and be in My presence.
To take your tears and exchange them for My joy.
To take your self-hatred and exchange it for My love.
I don't want anything from you, I want all of you.
I want all parts of you to experience My love, My joy, My
presence, My grace, My strength, My peace, My healing.
Only then will you find true rest.
Only then will you find true security.
Let Me be these things for you.
You did not earn it, but you're worth it.
I came to take your death and exchange it for LIFE!
I've caught you, and I'm never going to let you go.

DISCUSSION

It's easier to believe a lie than the truth sometimes. For me, discerning what is true about myself comes from the Bible. This is because those words do not change, and when my mind plays tricks on me or I can't remember what is true, I always have somewhere to go. Here are some of the verses and truths I find particularly helpful: Christ willingly died for me (Romans 5:8). Christ has taken on my pain that I may find healing (Isaiah 53:5). Christ took on my sin and has given me His righteousness (2 Corinthians 5:21). Through the Holy Spirit, I have peace (John 14:27). I do not have to be strong because He is strong (Philippians 4:13). Christ offers me hope (1 Peter 1:3). God wants to be with me (Psalm 46:10). My tears won't last forever, joy is coming (Psalm 126:5). I am loved by God (Isaiah 43:4). I can rest in Jesus; I don't have to do anything to be accepted (Matthew 11:28–30). I have done nothing to deserve grace, it is a gift, I don't have to work to repay it (Romans 5:6). Jesus gives my life meaning and purpose (Galatians 2:20). God is always with me (Deuteronomy 31:6).

Sometimes it is easy to believe these things, and sometimes it is a choice. One thing I have learned is that what is true about me cannot be based on how I feel in a particular moment. Feelings change and circumstances change. This is one of the reasons why I think truth is hard to find and hold on to. In a world where everything changes, it is getting harder to find and trust in something that doesn't change.

QUESTIONS FOR REFLECTION

Which of these statements or verses resonates with you the most? Why? Which of these statements or verses do you find hardest to believe? Why?

PRAYER

Breathe in, "Jesus." Breathe out, "Make Your truth real."

Take Me

Take me to a place
With no fear or shame.
Take me to a place
Where peace and love reign.
Take me to a place
Where I can be me.
Take me to a place
Where I am set free.
Take me to a place
Where hope and joy abound.
Take me to a place
Where I know I am found.
I know this place is not near or far—
It is wherever You are.
I cannot get there on my own,
Lead me to Your throne.

DISCUSSION

God's presence does not occupy a specific space. If you're like me, you know that, but sometimes it is easy to live like God's presence only occupies certain spaces. Places like churches or chapels or camps are obvious places of God's presence. Other spaces like small groups or times when God is invited to join are places where God's presence is expected. But the truth is, God's presence is not confined by walls or the types of activities that are taking place. I need to be reminded of this sometimes, because God's presence occupies the ordinary and even the dark places. He cares about what happens in those spaces. I have met God in a Walmart and on an airplane. I have also met God in a church building and on the floor of my room. When I ask God to make His presence known to me, He often does in the most unusual, mundane places.

QUESTIONS FOR REFLECTION

Where do you meet with God? What mundane or unusual place might God want to show you His presence in?

PRAYER

God, open my eyes. Show me that Your Presence is here. God, open my ears. Speak to me in the mundane places. Amen.

My Best Friend

My Best Friend has a name like no other.
His name is majestic.
His name is sweet.
He is the One who saved you and me.
I love Him and He loves me.
Dying on a cross is what He did—
The only way to find His house is if you ask Him in.
It isn't hard,
Just say a prayer,
And presto, He's there.
And what is the name of this Friend of mine?
As long as you promise to lift His name on high,
Jesus
Is all I can say.

DISCUSSION

I wrote this poem when I was 12 years old because that is truly how I felt about Jesus. And now over 10 years later, I find that this is still how I feel about Jesus. Not all the time, mind you, but often. As I reflect on my life, I see the presence of Jesus all over it, even in dark places that I still don't fully understand. My field of study is Children's Ministry, and I love that this poem describes what I believe to be the gospel message in such simple words.

I think the gospel gets overly complicated sometimes. What I love about children's ministry is that simple truths are profound. The gospel has been made understandable to little children by God (Matthew 18:3). It doesn't need to be complicated. The bottom line of my faith has not changed since I was 12—Jesus loves me, and I choose to love Him.

QUESTIONS FOR REFLECTION

How would you describe Jesus? What is the bottom line of your faith?

PRAYER

Thank You, God, for the relationship we can have with You. Bring us back to the simple truths when we forget and make things more complicated than they need to be. Amen.

Quiver and Quake

In awe and wonder, I stand
Overwhelmed by Your creation
Like a flood,
love and joy overtake me, and I
Quiver and Quake
Quiver and Quake.

Sitting here in Your presence,
You don't need me, but You want me.
Such a complex mystery
Yet You speak to me, and I
Quiver and Quake
Quiver and Quake.

On my knees
Broken by the weight of the world,
You died for me
To set me free, and I
Quiver and Quake
Quiver and Quake.

In the midst of turmoil and chaos,
In confusion, You bring clarity.
I am so guilty,
But I hear You whisper
"Forgiven."
I fall on my face, and I

Quiver and Quake
Quiver and Quake.

DISCUSSION

I grew up in a church where worship looked like singing, sometimes clapping, and for some people, raising hands. The time of worshipping through music in church services has always meant a great deal to me. I am a word- and emotion-orientated person, and so connecting with the words of a song and experiencing the emotions that follow certain rhythms and melodies in music helps me connect to God. This is not true of everyone, and it is not the only way to worship or connect with God.

This poem describes one of the more intimate ways I connect with God. The reason I share it is to show that there are many ways someone can connect with God. Ultimately, connecting with God can be a very personal thing. For example, I shake during worship. It first happened at a youth conference; I was sitting down, and my arms and my legs just started moving in my seat. My mind was totally at peace, and God was speaking to my heart in ways that I really needed to hear. Thankfully, there was a friend nearby who had had a similar experience. She not only walked me through what was happening when worship ended, but she also fielded all the questions people around me had.

Since then, if God wants to get my attention or if deep healing needs to happen in my heart, I shake. Sometimes it's just one hand, sometimes it is my whole body. And while this shaking brings me peace and reminds me of God's presence, I feel like an outsider in the church sometimes. In some churches, I'm too expressive, and in other churches, I am not expressive enough. I don't cry easily, and so I usually sit in the back so no one can see my dry eyes and my shaking limbs. I share this because when I sit in the back, I see other people like me who don't worship in a stereotypical way. And it's beautiful. God has given us each expressions of worship that are unique to our personalities and who He has made us to be. Worship in the way you were created to; you may encourage someone else.

QUESTIONS FOR REFLECTION

How do you worship? When was the last time you felt connected to God?

PRAYER

Lord, teach us how to worship. Thank You for the many different forms that worship takes. May You teach us to worship in the unique way You have created us to. Amen.

As I Walked

I walked along a dirt path
All alone,
But I didn't mind,
I was headed for the golden palace.
I had no reason to hide,
I passed other paths
I knew I wasn't supposed to take.
I stayed my course
And then the sun went dark.
Darkness swooped around me like birds of prey
And I became afraid.
I turned back,
I looked forward,
And running out of the golden palace came My Father.
He carried me in His arms,
He embraced me and held me close,
His embrace was safe and warm.
I started to walk again,
My Father right behind me
Sheltering me from the storm.
And every time I'd try to go too fast
He was always waiting for me to come back.
Then the darkness lifted,
The sun began to shine,
He threw me up on His shoulders
And we walked through a meadow—

A Daddy and His child.
We walked along the path.
One thing we never did was look back.

DISCUSSION

Maybe you have heard or read the story of the Prodigal Son (or the Lost Son) in Luke 15:11–32. In case you are not familiar with this story, let me give a brief synopsis. In this story, Jesus tells of a father who had two sons. The younger son wanted his inheritance before his father died. His father gave it to him, and the son left home and lost all his money in a string of bad choices. Left starving and homeless, the young son decides to return home and ask his father if he could be a servant because he was no longer worthy of the title "son." "But while he was still a long way off, his father saw him and was filled with compassion for him; he ran to his son, threw his arms around him and kissed him" (Luke 15:20, NIV). The father then threw a huge party for his son and welcomed him back into the family.

I have read this story many times, but one day when I was reflecting on it, I was struck with this image of a palace. I was standing on a path coming out of a forest, and the palace was off in the distance. And just outside the gates of the palace, Jesus was running to meet me. I sat with this image for a while and then wrote this poem. Three things struck me about this poem. The first is that in clear skies the palace did not seem that far off. At the end of the poem, I still had not reached the palace, and when the storm came, I could not see the palace anymore. There are times in my life when everything seems clear. I can see God's goodness and beauty and everything seems to be falling into place. Heaven has come down to earth and the end of suffering is believable, but while we are on this earth, there will always be things that happen that don't make sense. Suffering is real, storms come, and it is so hard to see the goodness and beauty of God in those times, much less believe it.

The second thing that struck me was, even though I was protected from the worst of the storm, I still tried to run ahead of Jesus. I think this is also true of life. When hard times come, we try to run ahead. We try to figure out why this is happening, why we are experiencing this pain, and once we find out why, we try to find out how. How did it happen? How can we get rid of it? How can we prevent it from happening again? We use our calendars as a way to keep moving at a frightening pace, because we think that if we do more, we will reach the end of all this chaos and pain faster. But what we are really doing by running ahead is adding to our own storm. When researching *why*, we find out all the *possible* reasons and start to worry that ALL of them apply to us. By researching *how*, we add more and more to our already overflowing calendars. And by keeping our calendars busy, we are not allowing our brains the chance to process all the pain and grief we are experiencing, thereby preventing healing. When I run back to Jesus, the pain doesn't automatically go away. The storm doesn't always end. But I stop adding to it. I have learned in my life to rest in the tension of the storm. To rest in the fact that Jesus is with me and yet I still experience pain. To rest in the fact that I won't always know why and knowing why won't take away my pain. To rest in the fact that I might come to the how eventually and I might not. And some days that makes me angry, and some days it makes me sad, and other days I'm ok. The answer to the storm is not to run ahead, but to keep going through it, even when some days that means shuffling my feet a few inches.

The third thing that struck me was that there was no looking back. This struck me because I wanted to look back. Even after the storm, I wanted to analyze it and understand it. I wanted to make sense of it. And sometimes it is important to look back. Sometimes there is healing that needs to happen, and it will only happen by first looking back. But sometimes we must rest in that tension again. Each situation is unique and different. I don't know where you find yourself on the path today. Wherever you are on the path, know this—for a path to exist, someone must have walked it before. You are not alone. If you are able, share your journey on the path so far. It might encourage someone else who is on a particularly steep incline or who has walked into the darkest forest.

QUESTIONS FOR REFLECTION

Read Luke 15:11–32. Who are you in this story? Where are you on the path right now? How can you take a step forward today?

PRAYER

Emmanuel, God with us. Remind us today You are with us on the path. Thank You for being with us in the tension. Help us to know Your presence, especially in the storm. Thank You for always welcoming us back to Yourself. Amen.

The Flame

Disoriented I stumble.
The smoke fills my lungs.
I cannot breathe and as I gasp for breath,
The roar of fire fills my ears.
My God, where are You?
All I feel is fear.
My God, can You hear me?
Why am I here?
Walls of fire surround me.
The flames are coming near.
How can I not respond in fear?
The anguish of my soul flows to my bones.
Unable to stand I kneel.
Unable to kneel I collapse.
I cannot fight these flames.
Despair has gripped my heart.
I wish I could cry but I can't.
Every breath is a whisper.
My God, do not forget.

DISCUSSION

Sometimes life is going well, and then out of nowhere it becomes so incredibly overwhelming, and nothing seems to make sense anymore. I wrote this poem during such a time in my life. Overnight it seemed like a violent storm cloud took residence over my heart, and it stayed for most of the year. My heart felt like it was going to beat out of my chest most of the time, and I didn't know where to go or what to make of it. When I prayed, it seemed like my prayers got lost in the smoke of the fire and were snuffed out before they left my lips. It was exhausting. It was around this time that I started to make a new spiritual discipline for myself.

I set a timer, close my eyes, and lie on the floor. Sometimes I pray, sometimes I let my thoughts wander, sometimes I still my mind, and sometimes I fall asleep. When everything seemed so out of control and I wasn't sure how I could keep stumbling forward, I found lying on the floor grounded my heart and mind (pun totally intended). There is something about having the solid floor beneath me, supporting me, that helps my mind calm down. I now call it my floor time with Jesus. It is my first response when things start to feel out of sync and out of control.

Lying on the floor is a physical reminder to my soul that I don't need to be strong all the time. It is ok to collapse. It is ok to let something else hold me for a while. And when I am on the floor, I am reminded that God is holding me; He has not forgotten me even if He feels distant. Here is the most important thing about my floor time, especially when I am feeling like I was when I wrote this poem—there is no agenda. I set the timer because if I fall asleep, I know I will wake up with enough time to do whatever I need to do and

I don't have to keep my eye on the clock. It is simply time to shut off all music and other noise and express myself to God, or hear from God, or rest. Most often it's a combination of all three. There is always ground beneath my feet and there is always a place to lie down, which is such a simple constant reminder that God is always present and is always available to listen and speak to my weary soul.

QUESTIONS FOR REFLECTION

What is out of control or overwhelming in your life right now? What is something simple you could make a spiritual practice?

PRAYER

God of Peace, it is hard to believe You truly do see and care in times of anxiety and confusion. Thank You that we can express our pain, anxiety, confusion, sorrow, anger, and whatever other emotion we may be feeling to You. Help us to find ways to remember Your presence, and when we are too tired and forget, thank You for not forgetting. Amen.

The Fire

The fire may surround me
But my God will not abandon me.
The flames may roar,
The heat may cause me to sweat,
The smoke may fill my eyes and my lungs,
It may feel like I am unable to breathe,
But my God, You have not abandoned me.
Even when I cannot see
You are with me.
Even when I cannot hear
Your love draws me near.
Even when all I feel is pain
My God, You do not speak in vain
And You promise to be with me.
I will not look at the flames;
I will not pay attention to their heat.
I will let Your whisper silence their roar
I will focus on You.
Because You promise
To be with me
Even when the flames surround me.

DISCUSSION

When the "fire" or anxiety or other hard circumstances last a long time, it can be hard to hear, see, and feel God's presence with you. Halfway through my "fire," I was reminded of the story of Shadrach, Meshach, and Abednego in Daniel 3. Let me provide a brief synopsis and share the hope found in this story. Shadrach, Meshach, and Abednego were Hebrew exiles who had become servants in the King of Babylon's palace. The king had built a statue of himself and commanded that when music was played, everyone must bow down and worship this statue of the king. Shadrach, Meshach, and Abednego refused to do so and were brought before the king. They were given another chance to bow down before the statue or be thrown into a blazing furnace. Shadrach, Meshach, and Abednego refused to bow down and were thrown into the furnace. Shadrach, Meshach, and Abednego were seen walking around in the fire with a fourth man who looked "like a son of the gods" (Daniel 3:25). Amazed by this sight, the king called for Shadrach, Meshach, and Abednego to come out of the fire. They came out completely unharmed and didn't even smell like smoke.

As I reflected on this story considering my own life, I thought, "Could that be true of me? Could I come out of this "fire" unharmed? Could whatever it was that was surrounding me really be prevented from consuming me and not touch me so that I wouldn't even smell like smoke?" And I wanted the answer to these questions to be yes. I knew there was nothing I could do to put out the fire, and for whatever reason, God wasn't putting it out either. I was overwhelmed and exhausted, but I decided that if I was going to walk through this fire, I wanted to be like Shadrach, Meshach, and Abednego. I wanted to be unbound. I was bound by the lies I kept feeding myself and that the enemy kept feeding me. Lies like God didn't care, the fire was too big for Him to get through, it was just my crazy emotions. Lies like I could have prevented the fire by being a better Christian, lies like I had to fight the fire on my own.

Maybe it's just me, but I have learned that my feelings lie to me a lot. What I feel is not usually what is true. And up until this point in my life, I assumed my relationship with God was good and real if it felt that way. After I wrote this poem, I realized all the truth that was in it, even though I didn't feel it. My relationship with God is not dependant on feelings. I could not have prevented the fire. I was not alone. What I was feeling and experiencing was real, I wasn't making it up. God cares about what I am feeling and experiencing. And as I spoke these truths to myself for months, slowly my feelings began to line up with that truth. Yes, I prayed that one morning I would wake up and the fire would be gone. That didn't happen. Gradually, as I listened and dove into what God said and chose to believe it despite my feelings, those feelings began to have less control over me. I can't pinpoint exactly when my "fire" ended because it just fizzled out over time. People were praying for me that the fire would end. I stopped praying the fire would end because I started to have conversations with God in the middle of the fire that were life-giving. Your feelings and your circumstances don't define you. God is present, God does care about you, God loves you, and God hears you, despite the fires you may be facing in your life.

QUESTIONS FOR REFLECTION

What lies have you been believing? What truth do you need to hear?

PRAYER

God who Delivers, we ask for Your deliverance from the fires and the lies going on in our lives. We ask for Your truth and Your presence to be made known to us. Help us to choose to believe truth and hear Your voice in times of despair, confusion, and anxiety. Amen.

In the Middle

I will bow
I will kneel
In the middle of the flames.
Not because I am afraid
Not because I am overwhelmed
But because I am in awe
Not of the fire
But of my Savior
Who is with me
Who could be anywhere
But chooses to stand in the flames.
His hands could hold down the flames
But He instead chooses to use
His mighty hand to gently pick me up.
One breath from His lungs could
Blow away all the smoke.
He knows how I long to see Him.
But instead, He draws me so close
That I can't help but see Him.
One word from His voice
Could silence their roar
But instead, He chooses to whisper
"I love you" right in my ear.
He knows when the flames will go away
But right now, there is no place I'd rather be.
Without the flames I wouldn't know
His sweet embrace

How ignorant I am to ask Him to move them when they
are the vehicle He uses to come near!
He is here;
He won't leave.
I'm not looking at the flames—
I'm looking at Him,
The One who has the power and authority
To put them out
But chooses to draw me close and
Whispers that I'm His child in my ear.
What a sweet noise the flames make
When they are forced to echo His voice.

DISCUSSION

Have you ever tried to blow out a candle while whispering?
I haven't been able to do it. Typically, to blow out a candle,
you need to stop what you are doing and blow it out. God
once said to me, "I'm not using My voice to blow out the
fire, I'm using it to speak to you." At that moment, I realized
that while I was begging God to do something, He was
already doing something else. He was wanting to wait out
the fire with me and speak to me. This caused me to learn
something about God. I learned God is the type of Father
who wants to sit with me, cry with me, and hear all about
my worry and frustrations. And meeting Him in the fire
did not answer all my questions. Could He have put the
flames out? I honestly don't know, but the answer isn't as
important to me anymore.

I recognize now that if He did put the flames out, I wouldn't have the relationship with Him that I do today. I learned to sit in tension. I learned to wrestle with God and express all my anger and frustration at the situation to Him. And even though it might not make logical sense, I came to see that I would rather serve a God whose desire is to sit with His children in their frustration and sorrow than a God who takes every pain away the moment we ask. This does not always make moments of pain easier, and I would be careful about telling that to someone who is experiencing great pain and loss. I also learned throughout my life that when I am in pain, I don't want someone to give me a theology of suffering. I don't want the platitudes of "everything happens for a reason" or "God's plan is always good," because sometimes life doesn't work out that way. Bad things happen and the course life takes us on just plain sucks.

When I am in pain, what I want and most often what I need are people to sit with me. People who will give me a hug and say, "I'm sorry life is so hard." I need people who will watch a movie and eat a bag of Miss Vickie's Salt and Vinegar chips with me. I need people who will play board games with me. I need people to just be with me. And so that's the course I've tried to take with others too. I have theories about suffering, but they are ultimately just theories. I don't know why bad things happen to good people. I don't know how to reconcile an all-powerful and all-loving God and suffering. And to be honest, I've given up trying to understand. What I do understand is that God sits with me when I feel so alone. When ministering to others, I try to do the same and say, "I don't know, but I'll wait out this storm or fire with you."

QUESTIONS FOR REFLECTION

When you are in pain, what do you want people to do for you? How might God be trying to make His presence known to you in your current suffering?

PRAYER

God who sits with us, pain sucks and life is hard. Living in tension is exhausting. Remind us today that You sit with us. You are no stranger to pain. The life You lived on earth was not easy. You are present in the tension. Teach us what it means to be with You in the fire and storms of our own lives. Amen.

Peacefully Broken

Hope
Is present
Even if there is only a sliver left.
Slivers have potential.
Hope—
Believing the impossible just might
Be possible.
Timid and shy
Slivers of hope rise,
Quiet and calm
Hearts shatter,
Each sliver given in love
To the Author of hope.
Possibilities are endless in Perfect Love's hands,
The journey of surrender
Slow,
Worthwhile.
Hope makes it possible to be peacefully broken.

DISCUSSION

Did you know there is beauty in your limitations? I think that's what being peacefully broken means. Being at peace with the fact that you have limitations, but that you also have worth and are capable of great things anyway. It's hard to admit you have limitations. In a culture where anyone can be anything and you can do anything you set your mind to, the options can be overwhelming. Because the truth is you can't be anyone, you can only be you, and that's a good thing. No matter how much I set my mind to it, I will not be the next world-renowned physicist because my brain just doesn't work that way. I am limited. And I have found that to be such a freeing thing. This doesn't mean that I accept all my limitations and stop trying to be better at certain things. That to me is what a sliver of hope is.

For example, I love writing and have been writing for years. I go through at least one journal a year, usually two. I have a whole shelf dedicated to old journals full of poetry, prayers, laments, and notes. Over time, some people read some of my writing and said they related to it; others told me I wasn't very good at it. I could have accepted that being good at writing would just be something outside of my reach, but I had a passion for it. There was this sliver of hope inside me that said, "Some people benefit from your writing, so go for it." And so, I did. I enrolled in a school that would teach me how to write and publish a book, I learned from peers and editors, and I am continuing to grow. It is a slow process and one that will never be completed, but it is so worthwhile. You will never be perfect on this side of heaven. We are all learning and growing. We are all limited, but even in our limitations, we are not alone, because God promises to teach us and complete the good work He began in us (Philippians 1:6).

QUESTIONS FOR REFLECTION

Where in your life do you feel limited? What is a sliver of hope in your own life? How can you grow in that area of your life?

PRAYER

God, thank You for limitations. Thank You for making us unique. Help us to have grace with ourselves and others; we are all works in progress. Complete the good work You began in us. Be our hope. Amen.

Drifting

Sometimes I feel like I'm drifting.
Drifting away or drifting towards,
I don't know,
I'm just drifting,
Coasting along hoping that where I'm going has meaning.
When I started out, the future was bright
I could see where I was going, and I was excited.
But now clouds have rolled over my destination
And I just don't know anymore.
Where am I going?
Somehow, I think I got turned around in the storm.
I'm not supposed to feel this way,
So my culture says.
The unknown is supposed to excite me.
So why am I so terrified?
The joy I once found in having no plan
Has been replaced by anxiety
That where I'm going may have no meaning at all.
Drifting
Through time and space
And I don't know when it will stop.
When will I feel something other than confusion?
Someone, please tell me I'm headed in the right direction.
There must be more to life than an empty plan.
I surrender the fragments of a dream into His hand—
The hand of the One who calmed the storm
The hand of the One who called me here.

He won't abandon me
I have nothing to fear
Even in my drifting, He is here.
He dreams bigger than I could.
I will trust the Son even though I can't see Him through
the clouds.
My drifting will come to an end.

DISCUSSION

I wrote this poem in the first week of my third year of college. Around my school, this feeling was known as "third-year apathy." I was assured by my friends (who were all a year ahead of me in school) that feeling apathetic and losing the ability to care about assignments and classes was normal in that third year. Maybe if you've gone to post-secondary, you know what I am talking about. However, for me it wasn't that I didn't care. The problem was that I did care greatly, but I was struggling to see the meaning in what a degree in Theology would actually do to help the world. I had just finished working at a summer camp where every day I was working directly with people, having conversations and doing work where I was rewarded with the smiles on the camper's faces. I knew what I did all summer had an impact. To go from that to sitting behind a desk again and writing yet another paper caused me to wonder why I decided to go to college at all.

Maybe you have had moments in your life where you feel like you are drifting. Not just because of school. Maybe you started a business, and at first, you were really excited, you saw all the potential, and now you are bogged down in the day-to-day logistics of your business. Maybe you started a new job and were excited to impart change in your workplace, but you're burnt out because of all the paperwork and office politics that plague your day-to-day. I've had moments in writing this book where I have gone, "What was I thinking?" It sounded like such a great idea, but now I have doubts. So, what do we do with these feelings? I finished college and I finished this book because in those drifting moments I reminded myself of why I started. I remembered the excitement I felt about beginning and kept looking forward. Sometimes we change course—I finished my degree in five years instead of four and I took a different route than I had expected to finish, but I still made my way to that finish line. And maybe if there was no passion when you started, it might be time to look at doing something new. Another thing I do in these moments is to remember that even in my drifting, God is present. I haven't drifted away from Him. And even if it is hard to know His presence, He is still there.

QUESTIONS FOR REFLECTION

Where in your life do you feel like you are drifting? How can you bring into your memory the passion you felt when starting? Do you need to try something new?

PRAYER

God who is with us in our drifting, would You part the clouds even a little bit so that we can know Your presence today? Renew Your passion in us, help us to finish what we have started. For those of us who need to change course, give us direction. Even if we cannot see the full picture anymore, give us the next step to take. Amen.

Forever

DISCUSSION

I am going to put the discussion before the poem today because this poem is a little bit different. It is a conversation between the reader (you and me) and God. There are six parts, three of the reader speaking and three of God responding. As you read this poem, feel free to make it your prayer or to change certain words to fit your context and what you are experiencing today. Yes, conversation with God can look like this. As you read this conversation I had with God one day, may it be an encouragement and an inspiration to you to have your own conversations with God.

(Reader)

No more hiding,
No more running,
I'm here.
No more prepping,
No more striving,
I'm here.
And I'm broken
And I'm hurting
And I'm lost
And I'm confused,

But no more sheltering,
I'm here.
The mask is off.
Here I am.
Do You still want to use me as a part of Your plan?

(GOD)

Absolutely I do
Because I love you
I've been waiting for you to stop—
To stop running
To stop hiding
To stop prepping
To stop striving
I'm here.
I always was.
I've seen you the whole time.
I know what lies beneath the mask
And I love it.
So just sit,
Let My presence sink in.
No more sheltering.
Silence
Joy
Peace
Hope
I give to you
Don't leave and come back for more.
Just stay with Me and it's yours,
Always
Forever.

(Reader)

But what about when I mess up?
When I've run too far,
Sheltered too much,
Prepped too long,
Hid so hard,
That I don't know myself, much less who You are?
When striving is all I know,
How can You say there is hope and peace?
When silence becomes darkness,
When joy is not present in my heart, thoughts, feelings,
or actions,
How can You say You're still there?
I want to believe
But I just don't understand
Why so much of my pain and torment isn't stopped by
Your hand.

(GOD)

Oh, My child
I know your pain and torment.
I felt it all at the cross.
I bore it in My heart.
I know exactly what you feel
And so much more.
Be patient and wait for what
The Father has in store.
I asked the Father to find another way, but there was
none.
I died to be near you,

That's how you know I'm here,
And even when you think I don't care,
I do,
And I love you too.
Joy isn't a feeling,
It's a choice
To believe My light is present in silence.
Darkness will not overtake you, My dear friend,
My Father will not let that happen.
Peace and hope are not emotions,
Rather they are things you choose to believe are present.
Striving is not all you know, because you know Me.
Get to know Me.
You can't mess up too much
You can't run too far
You can't hide for too long
You can't prep enough
To make Me stop loving you.
I will never regret dying for you
I will never wish you away from Me.
Please be with Me
Forever.

(Reader)

What You say is good and true
But often I don't know what to do.
I get so tired
I get so burnt out
That I forget Your truth.
I know You're here with me,
I really do,

But sometimes I forget You're inside of me too.
I don't want to be afraid,
But surrendering is hard.
I want to trust
But I'm not used to it.
Will You help me?

(GOD)

Of course, I will.
I've been waiting all along, for the invitation to open your
hands,
To open your eyes.
Give it all to Me,
All the good and all the bad.
I won't let go of your hand.
I am here to give you power and peace
To release everything
To Me.
I'm really here.
I really am.
And I really want your heart
And the things you hold onto with your hand.
When you forget,
I'm here to remind you
That I love you,
That I'm holding you.
I never burn out
I never get tired
So don't be afraid to give it all to Me.
I can handle it.
In fact, I already did.

Let Me be your wisdom,
Let Me be your strength.
I am with you
Forever.

QUESTIONS FOR REFLECTION

Which of these lines resonated the most with you? Why?
What do you need to say to God today? What is He speaking
in return?

PRAYER

Write your own conversation with God. Get out a blank sheet
of paper and start writing what you have to say to God. Write
all of it—praise, thanksgiving, sorrow, anger, questions, etc.
Then on a new line of the page write "God:" and ask God to
speak. Write down what you hear. Don't overthink this part.
Just write what comes into your mind as God's response. If
you have never done this type of exercise before, it might
take a while for your mind to silence itself so you can hear
God speak. That's ok, be patient with yourself. After you have
written down what God said, write a response and continue
going back and forth between you and God for as long as you
like. If you are nervous about hearing the "right" thing from
God, look back over what you wrote and ask yourself, "Does
this sound like the God I find in the Bible?" If the answer is
no, you can disregard it, and rather than being discouraged,
be encouraged that you are growing in discernment (being

able to hear the voice of God). Something I usually do is ask God to give me a verse or a passage that aligns with what I am hearing Him speak. God does not contradict Himself, so if it goes against something He has already said, it is not from Him. The simplest way to discern God's voice is to ask yourself, "Does this draw me closer to love?" "Does this make me want to love others more?" "Does this help me to love who God has made me to be more?" If the answer is yes, it is probably from God.

DAY SIXTEEN

New Horizons

Something new is on the horizon.
It's tempting to look back,
To dwell on what was
Or what could have been.
It's tempting to get stuck in the "what ifs."
But now I stand on a new horizon
Full of peace and deep contended joy.
It's tempting to look to the future,
To get lost in the "what ifs,"
To dream of what could be,
But then I would miss what is here
What is now
A new and beautiful horizon.
It brings no promise of peace or pain
Just an invitation
Like any other day
To surrender
The past and the future
To the One who stands outside of time.
Something new is on the horizon.

DISCUSSION

You know those moments in your life when everything about your day-to-day seems to be changing? The moment you graduated, the moment you started a new job, the moment you moved to a different city, the moment you entered a new relationship, etc. While something exciting and new is starting, something old is dying. The way things were before will never be again. In some cases, that is a relief, and in others, it is hard to let go and walk forward.

Sometimes we choose to change and sometimes change is thrust upon us. I find the times when change is thrust upon me are more difficult to walk into with peace and joy. For example, a worldwide pandemic changed the day-to-day life of everyone seemingly overnight. And I think we all know now that nothing will go back to "normal." I had to grieve the loss of the way things were and come to terms with a new normal and hold that normal loosely.

I'm not saying that I don't plan for the future or even dream about the future I want, because I do. I also spend time reflecting on the past, recounting good memories and learning how I would do things differently now. But I have found that too much time in the past or the future makes for a sad today. When I live in the moment, even the hard and painful ones, I find that each day is a little bit easier to handle. I know it's impossible to be in love with every moment of your life, and I know that it is impossible to make the best of every circumstance. Some circumstances suck and days are hard, and some moments are filled with sorrow, anger, and anxiety. I am suggesting that in each moment we take time to allow ourselves to be present. To be present in the joy before us. To be present in the sadness we might feel. To be present when our body says there is a reason to be anxious. To be present in peace and contentment. I have found that when I am present in these moments, God is present too. And when I ask for His presence in each moment, it is easier to not get lost in the "what ifs."

QUESTIONS FOR REFLECTION

Do you find yourself on a new horizon? How can you be present in each moment of your day today?

PRAYER

Breathe in, "Lord, be present." Breathe out, "In this moment."

Show Me

The walls are closing in,
I have lost all my senses.
Will I be able to breathe again?
I'm sure that no one will hear me
But I don't know what else to do.
So, I'll scream out of desperation—
Show me that You hear me
Show me that You're there
Take away this desperation
Show me that You love me
Show me that You care
Give me life once again.
I am a prisoner to my own mind.
I've tried and tried
But the lies win every time.
I don't know what truth is anymore.
Tears are coming to my eyes so I will cry—
Show me that You hear me
Show me that You're there
Take away this confusion
Show me that You love me
Show me that You care
Give me life once again.
When You come near,
The walls stand straight again.
I can breathe again.
When You are here,

The truth replaces the lies
That tried to destroy my mind.

DISCUSSION

I'll wager a guess that I'm not the only one who has felt like this. Sometimes these feelings last for a day, sometimes for weeks, and sometimes for months. Looking back on these moments, I find that my cry never was initially, "Lord, take away the pain" (that came later). My initial cry was always, "God where are You? God show me Your presence." I find that interesting because I wasn't trying to be super-spiritual. In fact, no one knew I was feeling this way or having these kinds of conversations with God.

I found that even if my feelings didn't change, there was something about releasing my frustration and my anger with feeling like God wasn't present that helped me to believe He was. I know that doesn't make a lot of sense. Choosing to believe God wasn't going to leave me and He values my honesty with Him gave me permission to express my emotions and my feelings. Expressing these emotions and feelings is what would eventually help them to come back into alignment with truth. The more I screamed, "God I feel like You're not here, but I want to believe it," the more I found my eyes were opened to see how He was present, and eventually the feelings followed. I also found great comfort in reading the Psalms. David is not afraid to express his emotion to God. And reading the account of his life in 1 & 2 Samuel shows that God didn't leave him or stop caring for him when he expressed those emotions. So, whatever you are feeling today, express it to God. Yes, even your anger and frustration and unbelief.

QUESTIONS FOR REFLECTION

What do you need God to show you? What is holding you back from expressing all your emotions to God?

PRAYER

Re-read the poem again and use your own words to express what you need God to show you.

Always

I am worried,
I am stressed,
I keep walking in shadows
In hope of finding light.
Sometimes I don't think
I'll make it through the night.
This is when I am reminded
Always You will guide me
Always You're right beside me
Always Your love prevails
Always Your grace remains
Always You think of me
Always You care for me.
When my faith is tested
When I can't withstand the pressure
When I'm lost and can't find my way
When my hope fades and only fear remains
I will believe the truth
Always You will guide me
Always You're right beside me
Always Your love prevails
Always Your grace remains
Always You think of me
Always You care for me
Never will You leave me
Never will You forsake me.

DISCUSSION

There are times in life when things are going well and it is easy to believe you are loved, cared for, and not alone. As I was reflecting on such a season of my life, I realized that the first thing I stop doing when I am entering a dark season is trusting and believing I am loved, cared for, and not alone. I wrote this poem as a reminder to myself in dark times. Sometimes the words bring encouragement, sometimes they bring more questions, and other times they are just the reminder I need to stop the lies and start living in truth again. The simple truth is this: I am never alone. You are never alone. And I know that does not answer all the questions, but it does mean you are never alone in your questioning. God loves you, always. God sees you, always. God cares for you, always.

QUESTIONS FOR REFLECTION

What truth do you need to be reminded of today? How does knowing you are seen, loved, and cared for impact the way you live or think?

PRAYER

God, thank You for being with us, always. Thank You for loving us, always. Speak Your truth over us and help us to believe it. Amen.

Defined

I'm broken, I'm hurting.
I have done wrong.
I'm not perfect.
I'm fearful and frightened.
Sometimes, I desire the admiration of other people.
Does this define me?
I'm not defined by what I do,
I'm defined by You.
I am not controlled by my past,
The King of kings has wiped it clean.
My future destiny is not my own,
It belongs to the One who made me.
I don't have a perfect past.
I wish I could change it.
I've hurt others, myself, and God.
I'm ashamed of who I was.
Everything reminds me of the past.
Does this define me?
I'm not defined by what I do,
I'm defined by You
I am not controlled by my past,
The King of kings has wiped it clean.
My future destiny is not my own,
It belongs to the One who made me.
If I can write my own story,
I can define myself.
I don't want to define myself any longer

Because I can't see past the brokenness.
Does this define me?

DISCUSSION

Identity. It's kind of a common word right now, at least in the church circles I run in. From a very young age, I've been taught that my identity is in Christ, but only recently did I start to ask, "What does that mean?" It's one of those things that gets said a lot but is never really talked about. When I tried to ask questions about what it really meant to "place my identity in Christ," I received answers like, "It means what you do isn't important, who you are is important." And I would respond with, "Ok, so if what I do has no meaning, I can do whatever I want?" And the response back would be, "Well, no. What you do still has value." And that would leave me thinking, "Oh, so what I do is important."

Confusing, right? Another response I often got was, "Who you are is more important than what you do." Ok, so who am I? And then people start throwing out phrases like "child of the King," "beloved," and "loved and chosen by God." And while these answers sound nice, they left me feeling like placing my identity in Christ meant losing my individuality. I felt like in order to live out my identity in Christ I had to let go of all the things that made me, me. I had to stop being introverted because Jesus talked to strangers. I had to stop asking questions because Jesus knew all the answers. And the most defeating of all, I thought I could never live out my identity in Christ if I felt sad because the fruit of the Spirit is joy.

Over time, I realized that, yes, while I am loved, while I am a child of the King, I am also still me. I have a unique personality: I like quirky movies, my perfect afternoon involves listening to *Adventures in Odyssey* (a kid's audio drama), and I can't stand small talk. The experiences I have had have moulded and shaped me in profound ways. I don't have to give up being introverted, being crazy analytical, or my questions to live out my identity in Christ. Past experiences and choices do not define me, but they do shape me. The future does not define me because it hasn't happened yet. Future choices and experiences will also shape me, but my identity will not be found in those choices. Finally, other people have no authority to tell me to change aspects of myself to be accepted by God. If my identity is in Christ, then it is in Christ, despite how I might be feeling or the decisions I may be making. God made me unique, and that's a good thing, so no I won't conform to a certain standard of identity. Identity is something each of us must wrestle with for ourselves. That is the beauty of placing our identity in Christ—we get to keep our individuality. I get to be me, and you get to be you.

QUESTIONS FOR REFLECTION

What defines you? What makes you unique?

PRAYER

God who made us, sometimes in our quest to place our identity in You, we forget that when You created us, You gave us a unique identity. As we strive to place our identity in something concrete, help us to not sacrifice the things You love about us, that makes us unique. Be with us as we wrestle to find our identity. Amen.

Come Find Me

You're feeling weary
You're worn out
Your heart is breaking
And tears fill your eyes.
In the evening
When you're tired and worn out,
Come find Me here.
In the morning
When you're hustling about,
Come find Me here.
Joy fills your soul
Hope has come to life
Your heart is full of scars
But healing and whole.
In the evening
When you're tired and worn out,
Come find Me here.
In the morning
When you're hustling about,
Come find Me here.

DISCUSSION

Think of this poem as a note from God to you. When I first wrote this poem, I remember it being a busy season of life. I felt like I was rushing from one thing to the next and couldn't keep up. I remember as I was getting ready one morning a thought popped into my head, "Come find Me here." I took it to be from God, because otherwise, it didn't make a lot of sense. As I got ready that morning, I started to talk to God about my day and how I had been feeling lately. I remember feeling more prepared to tackle all the things I needed to do that day, and it started a new habit in my life.

Every morning as I get ready, I talk to God. Sometimes I play music when I can't think of words myself, but most often, I think about my day, or certain people in my life come to mind, and I talk to God about it all. When I started to do this, it felt freeing because I realized that time with God did not have to be sitting in a certain spot, Bible and journal open, phone on silent for an hour. I am not a morning person, and I always strived to be someone who would wake up early to spend time with God. I slept in every single time. And I felt like a bad Christian because I couldn't get myself out of bed to spend time with Jesus.

I realized that morning that the guilt I felt did not come from God. God was willing to talk with me as I went through the routine of getting ready in the morning if I was willing to talk to Him. And since then, I talk to God at all sorts of random times throughout the day. When someone comes to mind, I pray for them. When I have a few minutes between tasks and don't know what to do for five to seven minutes, I talk to God about how my day is going or what I am feeling. My point in sharing all of this is to say that there is a time and a space for Bible study, and sometimes it means saying no to other things. However, God knows life can get busy and hectic sometimes, and the thought of opening your Bible is exhausting. It's ok. You can talk to God anytime, anywhere. Wherever you are, you can find Him.

QUESTIONS FOR REFLECTION

Where do you want to meet with God? When during your day could you talk with God while doing an ordinary task?

PRAYER

God who wants to be found, thank You for not being very good at hide and seek. Thank You that Your presence is not confined to a certain space or activity. Thank You that we can find You at any time and in any place. Remind us to look for You. Amen.

Joy

The joy of the Lord is your strength. Joy being strength?
How can it be? Joy is an emotion. It's fleeting. I can't
control if I'm filled with joy. I want to control my
strength. The joy of the LORD? What does that even
mean? I don't always feel God. I forget His presence. I
sin and do bad things. Certainly, God does not always
feel joy when He looks at me. Unless joy isn't an emotion.
Unless God is so much bigger and better than I could
possibly imagine. Unless God is joy. That is His character.
And I know that my God is strong. So, when He looks
at me, He sees His child, and that fills Him with joy.
Not because of what I have done but because of His
Son. Jesus' blood covers me and rights every wrong, and
because of that, I have joy. Because joy is a choice. It is not
an emotion. It is not a feeling. The joy of the Lord is my
strength because my God is strong, and when He looks at
me, He is filled with joy. My strength does not come from
myself, and neither does my joy.

DISCUSSION

There is a popular phrase used in churches and worship songs. The phrase is, "The joy of the Lord is my strength." This often-used phrase comes from the book of Nehemiah. Nehemiah comes right after the book of Ezra and before the book of Esther in the Bible. I first heard about Nehemiah when I was in Bible college. As I read and studied this book, I wondered why I had never heard a sermon preached on it. I was surprised when I found this joy of the Lord verse nestled in the middle of this book that isn't talked about a whole lot. Being that I was (and sometimes still am) a person who struggles to find joy, I was curious to see what the context of this verse was. What was it really saying? So let me give you some brief context for this often-quoted verse.

Nehemiah was a cupbearer to the king of the people who had led Judah into exile. At this point, Nehemiah and his people had been in exile for many years. The exile came as a result of the Israelites consistent disobedience and disloyalty to God. For more about the exile, read Jeremiah and 1 & 2 Kings in the Old Testament. While Nehemiah is in the service of this foreign king, he gets word that the walls of Jerusalem have fallen and the city is destroyed. This was significant not only because this was Nehemiah's homeland, but also because Jerusalem was thought to be God's chosen city. It was the place where the temple was, and the temple was thought to be where God's presence dwelt. The destruction of the city meant an absence of God's presence.

Nehemiah is distraught when he hears this news and begins to pray. He then receives permission from the king to go back to Jerusalem and rebuild its walls. Throughout the rebuilding phase and after, Nehemiah faces opposition and hardship. After the wall is rebuilt (you can read all about it in Nehemiah 2–7), Nehemiah says in Chapter 8 Verse 10, "Go and enjoy choice food and sweet drinks and send some to those who have nothing prepared. This day is holy to our Lord. Do not grieve, for the joy of the Lord is your strength." The Israelites then go on to celebrate what God has done and repent of their sins.

So, the joy of the Lord in this verse is not just about a feeling of happiness. It is not saying that if you have Jesus, you must be happy. It is talking about rejoicing in the grace of God and bringing yourself to repentance. As Christians, we have been made right with God through Jesus (2 Corinthians 5:21). And while this does bring joy, it does not mean life will be easy and pain-free. The joy of the Lord can be our strength to come to Him with whatever problem we might be facing. He rejoices over us with singing because He loves us (Zephaniah 3:17). I find it interesting that Nehemiah told the Israelites that the joy of the Lord was their strength before they repented. Nehemiah already knew what God's response would be. The joy that God has for you will be your strength to come to Him with anything and everything because He is ready to be with you.

QUESTIONS FOR REFLECTION

What does joy mean to you? How does knowing God rejoices over you even before you come to Him change your view of Him?

PRAYER

Breathe in, "Lord, I come to You." Breathe out, "Your joy is my strength."

Broken Dreams

I plan and I walk
I stumble and I fall
I'm sick of this disappointment.
You won't give up on me
So, I guess
I won't give up on You.

So here I am again
Another broken dream in hand
I didn't want this to be Your plan.
Here are all the pieces
Make them into something beautiful.
I want You to take me by the hand and be my guide
But in this moment, I want You to hold me
And let me cry.

DISCUSSION

We have all faced times when things didn't go as planned. Life took a sideways turn and now you are left holding the pieces of what you had hoped for. And the temptation in many Christian circles is to say, "God has a better plan." But honestly, I've held and seen too many broken dreams to believe that. I believe God redeems and restores, but I don't believe He destroys. I don't believe in a God who breaks and shatters. I believe in a God who heals.

And so, if you are holding a broken dream, let me invite you into the sacred conversation that goes something like this, "God, this sucks." You have probably heard Jeremiah 29:11, "'For I know the plans I have for you,' declares the Lord, 'plans to prosper you and not to harm you, plans to give you hope and a future.'" What you may not have heard is the context of that verse. Jeremiah is writing a letter to the exiles (the people who have been forcefully taken from their homes), and in this letter, God is telling the people to plant roots in their new country. He tells them in Verse 10 that they are going to be in exile for 70 years. If I am an Israelite, I am not a fan of this plan God has. I'm not seeing the hope and the future Jeremiah is talking about.

If I am being honest, sometimes in my life I don't see the hope and future Jeremiah is talking about either. It's tough to live in the tension of a loving God and so many broken dreams. I think humans have something called free will. Because of that free will, I do not believe God has a master plan for everyone's life, because that means if I make a wrong decision, I am outside of God's will. And I know I am not perfect, so I've already screwed up His plan. I do believe God guides us into better decisions, and sometimes there is a good choice and a great choice, and if we let Him, God will show us which is best. But I also think sometimes there are two equally good choices and God is saying, "Just pick one, I'm with you." And when things fall apart, I believe God is there too. When things fall apart before we pick ourselves back up and move on, I think it is important to sit and grieve with God. It is ok to be upset over what was lost. It's ok to cry when life throws you curveballs. God is not saying, "Hurry up, My plan is on a timeline." God is saying, "Let Me hold you while you cry, and we will pick up these pieces together."

QUESTIONS FOR REFLECTION

Do you believe God has a plan for your life? Why or why not? What do you do when a dream falls apart?

PRAYER

God of Redemption, help us. Help us know the difference between a good choice and a great choice. Help us trust You with the broken pieces of our plans. Make them into something beautiful. Thank You for not being the destroyer but for being the Healer and Redeemer. Amen.

Slow Down

Slow down
Slow down
I want to be with you.
Slow down
Slow down
I want to be with you.
My child,
Slow down
Breathe
Breathe deep
Encounter the light of My Presence.
My Presence is always with you,
But it is here
In the silence
You recognize it.
Slow down
Slow down
I just want to be with you.
Slow down,
My child,
Slow down
I just want to be with you.

DISCUSSION

Remember April 2020, about a month into quarantine due to the Covid-19 pandemic, when people were talking about how nice it was to slow down? Was that just something we said because we were trying to sugar coat the fact that Covid-19 completely disrupted everything we knew? Or was that the truth? Now that things are opening up again, I hear, "It's been a really busy week" or "I'm just so busy" all the time. I watch friends and family long for the weekend and a chance to slow down, only to fill the weekend with more activities. I am guilty of this too. But I find that when I take a second to stop and breathe, to be in silence for five minutes, my perspective changes.

Some days that five minutes of silence is hard to come by, other days it's easy. I used to think that the more I did for God the more God would love me and the more peace I would feel as a result. But when I realized that God cares more about being with me than He does about the things I do for Him, everything changed. It took me practicing this thing called "rest" to realize that God's love for me cannot increase. He already fully loves me. And yes, the silence can be uncomfortable at times. It can be scary to be with your own thoughts for a while. It may even be painful. But in those quiet slowed-down moments, God is so present and it is easier to be aware of it. I used to find it really hard to be quiet. But the more I practiced it, the easier it became, and now my moments of silence are life-giving. They remind me I am not alone. They remind me the God I serve wants to be with me.

QUESTIONS FOR REFLECTION

What does it mean to be "with God" to you? What is preventing you from slowing down?

PRAYER

Breathe in, "In this moment." Breathe out, "God is with me."

Anyone Else

Sometimes I lay awake at night, trying to slow down my
mind enough to sleep.
Sometimes I just want to scream, because maybe that will
stop the chaos in my head.
Sometimes I concentrate so hard on my breathing
because it is the only thing that seems stable.
Anyone Else?
Sometimes I reach for my phone to let someone in on
how I am feeling, only to pull away because I convince
myself I am an unfair weight.
Sometimes I look at my phone wishing, praying for it to
buzz, just to know someone is thinking of me.
Sometimes I wonder if I fell off the earth, who would
notice?
Anyone Else?
Sometimes I wonder why loneliness is breaking my heart
when I KNOW I am not alone?
And then I tell someone that and they give me that "it's
in your head and not your heart" speech,
And that leaves me so defeated because my knowing goes
deeper, it does,
But the crippling feeling of loneliness is still there.
Sometimes I wonder if something is wrong with me and
it can't be fixed on this side of heaven.
Anyone Else?
Sometimes I repeat to myself over and over it's going to
be all right

And I believe, but I don't feel it.
And someone tells me to have more faith, and I just want
to punch them in the face.
Anyone Else?
And maybe I'm writing this letter to no one.
Maybe I'm the only one who lies awake at night and
thinks, "Again, I have to battle all of this again?"
But I'm willing to bet someone will read this and say,
"I've been there too."
We are in good company.
I like to think that some of the Prophets may have had
similar nights.
Of course, there is no way to know for sure.
But Jeremiah was thrown into a well after years of
Preaching God's message.
A message he wrestled with God about for years.
I'm willing to bet he had lonely nights too.
I find my hope like he did,
Through lament and trust,
Lamenting in my circumstance and trusting in my God.
Anyone Else?

DISCUSSION

Life is hard, and it can be lonely. The feelings and thoughts we have are unique, and the way in which we process them is equally unique. If you answered "yes" to any of the statements above, you are not alone, and there is hope for you. I love the book of Jeremiah. Not because it is easy to read but because I see Jeremiah's humanity so strongly as he lives out the calling God placed upon his life. Jeremiah also wrote the book of Lamentations, which is very relatable if you have ever walked through seasons of sorrow or grief. As I read Jeremiah, I see that he wasn't afraid to express himself to God. He understood that lament was a holy practice, just like rejoicing. And for all that Jeremiah went through, he still chose to follow God. I don't think he had all the answers, because if he did, I am sure he would have shared them in his book.

It is ok to have questions. God can meet you there. If you resonate with any of the lines in the poem, can I encourage you to reach out to someone? I know it is scary, but you are not an unfair weight. You have value, and your feelings are real. I can't promise you will be understood, but more often than not, people are just trying their best. The problem is not your faith. God is no stranger to sorrow. He can handle your questions.

QUESTIONS FOR REFLECTION

What is your own question where you are asking, "Anyone else"? Where do you find hope?

PRAYER

Breathe in, "I am not alone." Breathe out, "I have value."

Sad Eyes

The light in my eyes is gone.
I smile, but in my eyes,
There is only a blank stare—
Lifeless
Stoic
Tired.
The mask doesn't hide the eyes.
I can't fake joy.
My eyes were learning to dance again,
Their colour radiated with life.
That same colour seems to be faded now.
I don't know how I lost it
And I can't bring it back.
Who will look into my eyes and say,
"I love you"
When there is no sparkle in return?
Bring my sad eyes to life once more,
Make them dance again!
Speak the words,
"I love you"
Until the ice around them breaks
And the tears fall.

DISCUSSION

Have you ever looked into a mirror and noticed your eyes? I mean, really noticed them? Maybe it is because the bottom half of my face has been covered for most of the past year, but I find I am paying more attention to my eyes. No matter what facial expression I choose, my eyes portray what is going on inside. When I am doing well, my eyes seem brighter. When I am having a hard day, my eyes seem cold and distant. And I like what they look like on a good day because they are alive and seem to dance. I cannot fake the sparkle and I cannot force joy if it isn't there. When my eyes are lifeless and stoic, I want to do something to bring the sparkle back. But the truth is feelings come and feelings go, sometimes with no particular reason. All I can do is rest in what I know to be true and remind myself that if my eyes danced once, they could dance again. The ice around them always breaks eventually, and the smallest sparkle returns and grows.

QUESTIONS FOR REFLECTION

Have you ever noticed emotion in your eyes? What does a healthy release of emotion look like for you?

PRAYER

God who sees, show us that we are loved, even if we have sad eyes. Bring to life once again the eyes that have gone lifeless. Help us to break the dam of emotion so that they can dance again. Amen.

Lament Is Worship

Lament and grief
They seem all too prevalent right now
And the temptation is to push them away,
To resort to happier things.
The only problem is that doesn't change the deep sadness
inside.
No amount of smiles can take the pain away.
The problem isn't that you've stopped believing,
The problem is you are believing—
Believing things are not supposed to be this way,
And you are right.
Somehow, we got this idea that lament and grief are
inadequate forms of worship.
We know we can bring our lament and grief to God,
But they feel like burdens,
And burdens are no gift for the newborn King.
But what if lament and grief are forms of worship?
What if lament and grief are among the purest forms of
worship?
God does not want our fake smiles,
He does not need our fake smiles.
When we lament before God
And offer Him our grief,
We are giving Him our whole selves
Saying "God make this right."
And then like the Prophets, we wait
We lament

And we grieve
And we wait.
And through it all what if God is saying,
"I'm here, thank you for this gift"?

DISCUSSION

Christmas, the time of year when everyone is singing happy songs and decorating their houses with lights. I love Christmas. I love finding the perfect gift for someone, I love playing all the Christmas music, I love decorating the house and driving around the neighbourhood looking at Christmas lights. But a couple of years ago, Christmas felt different. It was hard. I didn't have to look very hard to see the pain and grief the world was going through. I found myself listening to the lyrics of "O Come, O Come, Emmanuel" repeatedly. The word "Emmanuel" means "God with us." Really, the song is a lament about waiting for God to come and be with His people again. And that's what I felt the world was waiting for. Waiting for God to show up in all the places where our world was falling apart.

I believe God is with us, and Christmas is usually a time where I reflect on how God has been present in my life over the past year. But this particular Christmas I found myself reflecting asking, "God, where are You?" And then I remembered the prophets. I remembered there was a whole book in the Bible about lament. I remembered that David wrote Psalms out of lament and grief and God never turned any of them away. And so, I began to lament and grieve before God as a form of worship.

Fast forward to the following Easter, the issues of the world had not been resolved. I identified greatly with Good Friday and Holy Saturday, the days meant for lamenting and waiting. Come Easter Sunday, I could not join in the celebration. Joy wasn't something I could express yet. And while I felt very out of place Easter Sunday, I found God later that afternoon on the floor as I lamented and grieved. I played "O Come, O Come, Emmanuel" because it was still the cry of my heart. And in that moment, I knew I was accepted and loved, and God did not despise my offering of worship.

QUESTIONS FOR REFLECTION

What gift can you bring to God that may be seen as "unworthy"? What is your song of lament?

PRAYER

O Come, O Come, Emmanuel. And redeem the broken things of this world. We bring before You our lament and our grief, You God will not despise (Psalm 51:17). We choose to rejoice, because Emmanuel, You have come. Amen.

Doubt

Questions and answers
Wrong and right
This or that
Us or them—
It all seems so simple,
Except when answers give way to more questions
Except when right and wrong aren't so clear
Except when I don't want this or that
Except when I want us to be like them.
It's safer to believe in a world
With straight lines and well-defined boxes,
But life twists and turns and sometimes it feels like I am
going in circles
And I realize all the boxes I've made
And those that have been given to me
Are way too constricting.
It's hard to live in tension,
It's hard to not know,
But that is where I have found freedom.
You only have the freedom to ask questions
If you have first given yourself the freedom to say, "I don't
know."
Life and faith are mysteries
Wrestling with God in tension.
I always find Him here
Because there is no way He fits into a well-defined,
constricting box.

DISCUSSION

I have a degree in theology, and I must say that I have more questions now than I did before I started school. The more I learned about God and the Bible, the more I began to see that there is so much we as humans do not and cannot know. At first, this bothered me. I searched for answers, and I tried to live my life by a list of hard and fast rules so that I always did what was right. And I realized one day, while I had found some answers, what I really found was a relationship with God I didn't know I was allowed to have. I began to sit in the questions and the "I don't know" and was ok if I never found the answer. I began to see that the world is really grey and there are loopholes everywhere. And while this was overwhelming at first, I began to find freedom when I let all the boxes go.

There is a story in Genesis 32:22–30 where a man named Jacob wrestles with God. I have always loved this story because Jacob was not a perfect man, yet he wrestled with God and God blessed Him. I love this story because it wasn't Jacob's righteousness or good behaviour that got him close to God. I don't know exactly what prompted this supernatural wrestling match, but I do know that when I have doubts and questions, it feels like I'm wrestling. Wrestling for answers and wrestling for truth. This story took on new life for me fall of 2021 when I realized that in order to wrestle with someone, you must get really close to them. When you and I wrestle with God, we must be close to Him, we are close to Him. I don't think we should stop looking for answers. I do think we should express questions and doubts. I have found that I enjoy the process of finding the answer more than the answer itself. Doubts, questions, and mystery are all vehicles that can bring us closer to God.

QUESTIONS FOR REFLECTION

What doubts or questions do you have? How can you wrestle for answers?

PRAYER

God who does not fit into boxes, thank You for not being confined and constricted by systems that are flawed. Thank You for wrestling with Jacob and for wrestling with us. Help us to give ourselves the freedom to say, "I don't know" and the freedom to ask questions. Amen.

Wake Up

Wake me up when it's over,
Wake me up when the judgement is gone,
Wake me up when fear is no longer king,
Wake me up when there is peace.

I am calling you to wake up now.
Yes, while there is still chaos and fear,
Wake up.
I'm redeeming all the frustration you see
Because I am still King,
Wake up.
Stop trying to control everything and listen—
Listen to My voice,
Listen to My heartbeat.
I am speaking peace—
Peace over your weary soul,
Peace over your overthinking mind,
Peace.
Wake up.
Take My hand,
Join Me in restoring what was lost.
I won't force you,
I know it's hard.
Just wake up and see
I am all that you need.

DISCUSSION

Maybe you can relate to the first four lines of this poem. Sometimes I just want to go to sleep and wake up when the world is a better place. It was on such a day when God invited me to wake up. Not in a passive way by just acknowledging the good things (although that can be a good practice), but in an active way. The result is the poem you just read. I came to realize that if I wanted to wake up one day to a better world, I needed to become an active participant in God's work of redemption.

The theme of redemption and restoration is woven throughout the Bible, and it is the main reason why I am still a Christian. I see how throughout history God has redeemed and restored, and I believe He is still in the business of redemption. And the cool thing is that He invites each one of us to join Him. Not because He needs us, but I believe redemption does happen faster when God's people are willing to join Him in whatever capacity they are able. Some days I can give a lot and some days I utter the prayer "Oh God" over and over. Sometimes I get caught up thinking I have to do something big in order to join God in His work of redemption, but on a day-to-day basis, I have come to realize the small things are just as important. If God gives you a big dream, do it! Rally people around you who will support you and believe in it and shoot for those stars. If God gives you a small random act of kindness, do it! Even if it seems strange and silly. That random text, song suggestion, coffee, or smile may just make someone's day. You never know what dreams you are inspiring or what hope you might be offering. And we could all use some extra hope.

QUESTIONS FOR REFLECTION

How might God be calling you to wake up? How can you join God in His work of redemption today?

PRAYER

God of Restoration, help us to wake up. Give us dreams of how to join You as You redeem this world. Renew our hope. We need You. Amen.

The Tapestry

My life was a work of art
A tapestry
Carefully woven.
It was not the most beautiful picture,
But it was mine,
And with it, I was accepted
I was proud of my tapestry,
And others were too.
Until one day—
The day I realized I am not a master weaver.
I had made this tapestry on my own and I had left a loose
thread
And one day it got pulled
And the whole picture began to unravel.
I panicked and I cried as the tapestry became a ball of
yarn at my feet.
I had worked so hard to present the right tapestry and it
was all coming apart.
And then I heard a voice,
"Can I have some more thread?"
And as I turned around, I saw a Man weaving a tapestry
out of the ball of yarn at my feet.
He could sense the confusion in my eyes and said,
"Don't worry, when I weave a tapestry, it never falls apart.
I am taking all the things that were a part of your tapestry
and putting them in their place. Your life is going to be
one of My great masterpieces."

I handed Him the thread and backed away
In awe of what He had just said.
And to my surprise, He called me back.
"I weave at your pace," He said, "You give Me the thread
and I weave, and when you need a moment to process or
cry, I'll take a break and hold you."
Numbly I nodded and began to give Him the thread
And to my horror, I looked back and saw what remained
of my tapestry continue to unravel.
But as I looked back at the Master Weaver again, I
realized
For my life to become a masterpiece
What I had strived to build needed to come down,
And my soul was filled with grief and peace.
We stood in silence until I asked,
"Why doesn't my tapestry look like a masterpiece?"
"This is the back of it," He explained. "Trust Me, the front
will be beautiful, but you have to wait until it is finished
to see it."
And so, in anticipation, I continued to give Him the
thread.
Sometimes we talked as He wove
Sometimes we stood in silence
Sometimes we stopped for a good cry
And sometimes we were forced to stop from laughter.
I became friends with the Master Weaver
And I can't wait to see my tapestry.

DISCUSSION

I am not an expert at making tapestries, but as I was reflecting on my life and some big questions one day, I began to imagine this scene so clearly in my mind. I realized that for most of my life I had tried to present myself in the "right" way. I believed in the "right" things, I acted the "right" way, and I did what people expected of me. But one day I went, "This doesn't fit." I was asking some big questions, and the "right" answer didn't seem so right anymore. I began to tear down the picture I had created because I didn't believe in a lot of it anymore.

This process was terrifying because as I worked with God to rebuild my worldview and view of Him, I realized that I no longer fit. I didn't fit in the communities I had been a part of in the way I thought I was expected to I guess that's the second part of my tapestry, learning that I don't need to apologize for the things that make me, me. As I continue to let God weave my story, I see how He is redeeming every part of it, and I am becoming more like Him in the process. It's a process I know will last the rest of my life, and sometimes the tapestry doesn't look so good, but then I am reminded that at the end there will be no loose threads. This one will not crash down on me. I have also found a community where I fit. Where I can be me with all my questions and all my quirks and be accepted.

To those who are facing the "this doesn't fit" moment and the tapestry is beginning to unravel, there is a place for you in the Kingdom. You are loved. You are seen. This is not the end. To those of you who are saying "I don't fit," there is a place for you in the Kingdom. We are all welcome to come to God to receive life and hope. I pray you find a community where the love of God is made manifest to you by His people. I thought I didn't fit for a long time until I realized I fit perfectly in the arms of Jesus.

QUESTIONS FOR REFLECTION

Has there been a time when a "loose thread" was pulled in your life? Are you willing to give Jesus the messy ball of yarn and join Him in weaving your tapestry?

PRAYER

Master Weaver, when what we have built begins to fall apart, it hurts. It sucks. Thank You for being a God who holds us in our grief before helping us give You the pieces. In this process of tearing down the things that don't fit and finding You in mystery, help us to be patient with ourselves. When we feel like we don't fit, help us to remember You always have a place for us. Thank You for being the Master Weaver who is patient, kind, and oh so loving. Amen.

A Letter to Those in Waiting

To those in waiting,

Those waiting for a dream
Those waiting for a letter
Those waiting for a child.
Those waiting for a boyfriend or a girlfriend
To those waiting for a friendship
To those waiting for hope
Those waiting for grace
Those waiting for joy
Those waiting for tears
To those waiting to feel, anything
To those waiting to travel
To those waiting for adventure.
Those waiting for a calling
Those waiting for a call
Those waiting for an e-mail.
To those in waiting for anything
To those in waiting for everything
To those waiting for a home.
Those waiting not to be alone
Those waiting for a reason to smile
Those waiting for a reason to live.
I'm sorry.
I'm sorry you have been waiting so long.
Because the truth is whether you have been waiting for
days, months, or years, waiting sucks.

Waiting is hard.
The thing for which you wait is out of your control, but everyone around you expects you to be in control.
The truth is you can't control why you wait.
And I won't tell you to be patient because that is what everyone tells you.
There's a reason for your waiting.
But to hear that while in the middle of waiting is like explaining the benefits of water to someone who is drowning.
You already are overwhelmed.
Consumed by false guilt.
So let me be the one to sit beside you as you cough and gasp for breath.
Breathe.
I know it hurts.
I know you feel disappointed.
You feel unheard.
You feel frustrated.
But I want you to know you are not alone.
I want you to know that that for which you wait does not and will not define you.
I don't come with a solution.
I cannot make you feel better, or make the pain disappear.
I can only challenge you to be honest.
Be honest about how the wait is.
Those who wait need to stand together
Not in judgement or shame but in unity,
Dismantling the lie that waiting is selfish.
Please be honest with your pain.
Those around you can't love you well if they don't know your hurts.

So please be honest.
Dare to be vulnerable in this moment—
Someone is waiting for you.
Yes, you.
They are waiting for your story
Waiting for your struggle
To stand with you
To be encouraged by you
To embrace you.
I don't know what it is for which you wait,
I wish I could promise the wait will come to an end soon,
But I can't.
And so, I offer you an invitation
To be honest,
To be unashamed.
One more thing, please don't stop waiting. To stop
waiting is to only give up on yourself.
—Someone who waits.

QUESTIONS FOR REFLECTION

What are you waiting for?

PRAYER

"The Lord bless you and keep you; the Lord make his face
shine on you and be gracious to you; the Lord turn his face
toward you and give you peace" (Numbers 6:24–26).

ACKNOWLEDGMENTS

Special thanks to my Mom and Dad for raising me to believe in myself and for all the support you have shown in this writing process. A huge thank you to the bestest littlest sister ever, Marisa. Ris, you truly are my number one fan and always know how to keep me going. Thanks to my cousin Jamee who may not realize it, but is my biggest inspiration for this book. No one encourages me to go for my dreams as you do.

Also, a big thank you to my editor Sky, as well as my formatter and cover designer Lucy Holtsnider, who gave me constructive feedback and worked with me to help fulfill my vision for this book. Thanks to my amazing friend and photographer Abbey @abrowingphotography. Thanks to Tiff for proofreading my manuscript, I appreciate all your encouragement and feedback. A huge thanks to my SPS coach Ellaine and the Mastermind Community, this would not have been possible without you!

A special thanks to my mentor and friend Kiara, who read almost every poem shortly after it was written and listened to my heart, no matter what state it was in. I would not be where I am today without you. Big thanks to all my friends and family, especially Abbey, Amy, Tiff, and TJ who were always so excited to hear updates and provided more support and encouragement than I ever could have asked for. To all the other people in my life I do not have room to thank, thank you. Thank you for buying the book and promoting it and helping me achieve my dreams.

ABOUT THE AUTHOR

Sara Katarina lives just outside of Edmonton, Alberta, where she graduated from Vanguard College with a Bachelor of Theology in Children's and Family ministry, minoring in Intercultural Studies. She loves asking tough questions and uncovering the answers. For her, the joy is in the process of finding an answer, not in the answer itself. Sara lives and loves with the conviction that people are accepted and valued for who they are and is passionate about sharing this truth.

THANK YOU FOR READING MY BOOK!

I hope you were encouraged and inspired as you read it. As I write more books in the future it is important to know what you thought! Please leave me an honest review on Amazon letting me know what you thought of the book. I would love to hear from you and if you would like to stay up to date on my next project you can sign up for my e-mail list at authorsarakatarina.weebly.com or find me on Instagram @authorsarakatarina

Thanks so much!

Sara Katarina